my
CAT
MANDALA
COLORING BOOK

C&T PUBLISHING

Another Maker Inspired!

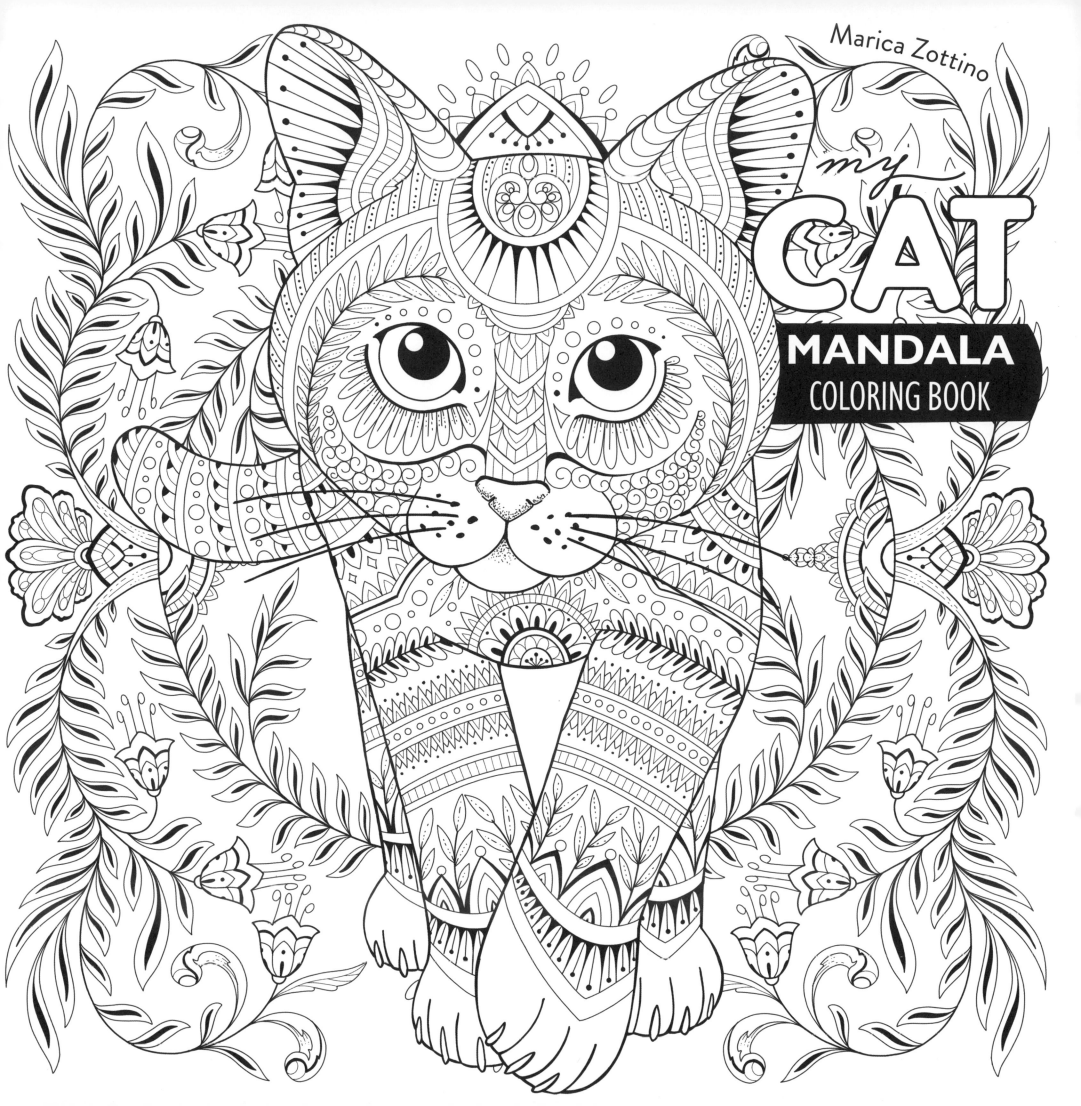

"You never choose a cat; it's the cat that chooses you."

Philippe Ragueneau

"If you are worthy of its affection, a cat will become your friend but never your slave."

Théophile Gautier

"Cats are beings made to store caresses."

Stéphane Mallarmé

"I like cats because I like my home. And little by little, they become its visible soul."

Jean Cocteau

"Spending time with cats, you only risk enriching yourself."

Sidone-Gabrielle Colette

"The cat practices its vigilance where no one can see it: in its heart."

Confucius

"Let's go to sleep, little black cat. [...] We will sleep, paws in arms."

Charles Cros

"I like in cats that independent and almost ungrateful character, which

makes them attach themselves to no one, and that indifference

with which they go from sitting rooms to their native gutters."

François-René de Chateaubriand

"Nothing is sweeter, nothing gives one's skin a sensation more delicate, more refined, more rare than the warm and vibrating coat of a cat."

Guy de Maupassant

"The cat is beautiful; he imparts notions of luxury, cleanliness, voluptuousness ..."

Charles Baudelaire

"I believe cats to be spirits come to earth. A cat, I am sure, could walk on a cloud."

Jules Verne

"Ambition is like the cat, who likes to be pet on the back."

Anne Barratin

"The sensual instinct is like a cat that sleeps and must never be awoken."

Henri-Frédéric Amiel

"The ideal of calm is in a seated cat."

Jules Renard

"The dreams of cats are inhabited with mice."

Lebanese Proverb

"It is difficult to catch a black cat in a dark room, especially when it isn't there."

Chinese Proverb

"White cat, without a mark,

I ask you, in these lines,

What secret sleeps in your green eyes,

What sarcasm beneath your whiskers."

Charles Cros

"At night, all cats are gray."

"I am the cat that basks. As soon as the sun passes over."

Henri Monnier

"Cat's game, mouse's tears."

Russian Proverb

"Cats move as silently as though they were treading on air or walking on clouds."

Natsume Sōseki

"God has made the cat to give man the pleasure of caressing the tiger."

Victor Hugo

"Don't give a cat anything just because it's meowing."

French Proverb

"The cat went here and there. The moon spun round like a top."

William Butler Yeats

"There is no cat so small that it will not scratch."

French Proverb

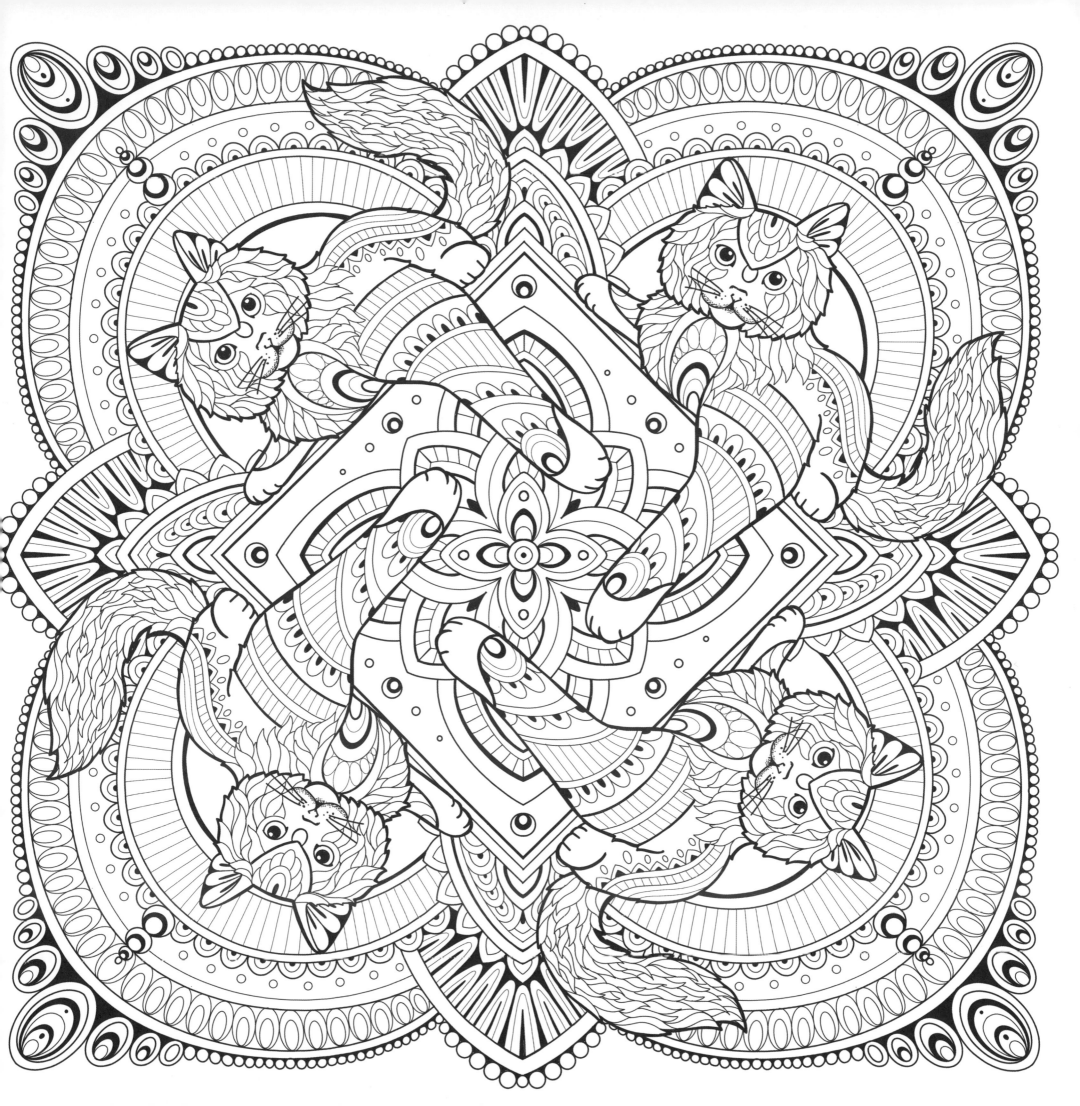

"A house without a cat is an aquarium without a fish."

Jean-Louis Hue

"I want in my house [...] A cat moving among the books."

Guillaume Apollinaire

"I am the cat of misfortune, the troublemaker in the moonlight."

Henri Monnier

"I am a cat. I don't have a name yet. I have no idea where I was born.

The only thing I remember is meowing in a dark and damp place."

Natsume Sōseki

"Time spent with a cat is never wasted."

Sidonie-Gabrielle Colette

My Cat Mandala Coloring Book

First published in the United States in 2023 by C&T Publishing, Inc., P.O. Box 1456, Lafayette, CA 94549

© First published in French by Rustica, Paris, France—2021

This edition of *"Mes Mandalas Chats à Colorier"* by Marica Zottino first published in France by Éditions Rustica in 2021 is published by arrangement with Fleurus Éditions.

PUBLISHER: Amy Barrett-Daffin

CREATIVE DIRECTOR: Gailen Runge

SENIOR EDITOR: Roxane Cerda

EDITOR: Jennifer Warren

ENGLISH-LANGUAGE COVER DESIGNER: Julie Creus

ENGLISH TRANSLATION: Kristy Darling Finder

PRODUCTION COORDINATOR: Zinnia Heinzmann

ILLUSTRATOR: Marica Zottino

ISBN 978-1-64403-356-2

Printed in China

10 9 8 7 6 5 4